a year in the life of the eden valley val corbett

F

FRANCES LINCOLN LIMITED

PUBLISHERS

a year in the life of the eden valley val corbett

Acknowledgements

I found two books invaluable – Michael Ffinch's informative *The Upper Eden Valley*, and Charlie Emett's excellent read, *The Eden Way*. I am indebted to the East Cumbria Countryside Project (sadly no more) and in particular Dick Capel, for entrusting me with a variety of pleasurable photographic commissions, enhancing my appreciation of the Eden Valley. My thanks go to Tim Longville, for casting his beady eye over a draft of the Preface to this book – and telling me to start again! We remain friends. I commend working with Maria Charalambous and Nicki Davis of Frances Lincoln, both for their expertise and for their lightning quick responses to emails.

My greatest thanks are reserved for my husband Tony, from whom I ask the world, but gives me more.

HALF TITLE PAGE **On the shortest day of the year the sun sets in a direct line across the valley down High Cup Nick.**

TITLE PAGE **The late evening sun streams across the relatively level valley floor near Ousby.**

RIGHT **These cornfields, crossed by a footpath leading to Wetheral, are a typical creation of late enclosures. Large areas of the outer fringes of the ancient Inglewood Forest, which covered a vast area of the western side of the Eden Valley, were cleared for agriculture.**

Frances Lincoln Limited, 4 Torriano Mews, Torriano Avenue, London NW5 2RZ www.franceslincoln.com

A Year in the Life of the Eden Valley
Copyright © Frances Lincoln Limited 2010
Text and photographs copyright © Val Corbett 2010

First Frances Lincoln edition 2010

978-0-7112-3015-6

Printed and bound in China

1 2 3 4 5 6 7 8 9

contents

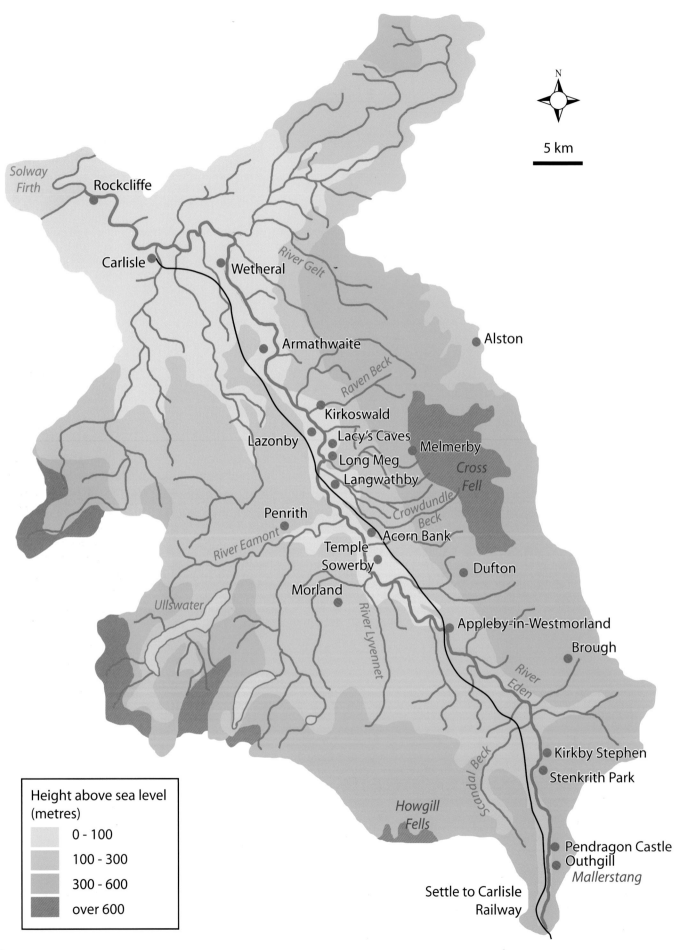

N

5 km

Solway Firth

Rockcliffe

Carlisle

Wetheral

River Gelt

Armathwaite

Alston

Raven Beck

Kirkoswald

Lacy's Caves

Lazonby

Long Meg

Melmerby

Cross Fell

Langwathby

Crowdundle Beck

Penrith

Acorn Bank

River Eamont

Temple Sowerby

Dufton

Morland

Ullswater

River Lyvennet

Appleby-in-Westmorland

Brough

River Eden

Scandal Beck

Kirkby Stephen

Stenkrith Park

Howgill Fells

Pendragon Castle

Outhgill

Mallerstang

Settle to Carlisle Railway

Height above sea level
(metres)

0 - 100

100 - 300

300 - 600

over 600

the eden valley introduction

My house faces east and, although a map shows that I live just within the boundary of the Lake District National Park, the distant view from our windows is to Cross Fell rising above the Eden Valley. When selecting photos for this book, I noticed for the first time how integral to the Eden Valley that soaring outline of Cross Fell is, how one's eye is constantly drawn to it and what a splendid backdrop its great bulk makes for the patchwork of fields in the valley. Cross Fell, or Fiend's Fell as it is traditionally known, also marks a division between the far north-east and north-west of England. In Cumbria only one road crosses from east to west over the wild backbone of the Pennines. Travelling westwards through Alston this dramatic route, frequently snow-bound in the winter, rises to Hartside summit where a magnificent prospect of the Eden Valley is spread out below with the Lake District fells rising beyond. A long series of hairpin bends then descends from the wild uplands. The scenery softens and the first Eden Valley village of Melmerby is reached, one of the chain of little fellside villages securely tucked at the feet the Pennines. From here the road straightens out through farming country, passing sandstone barns and dry stone walls, until it reaches the River Eden. Along the river's course are the larger villages and small market towns of the Eden Valley.

The great benefactress, Lady Anne Clifford, erected a sturdy pillar marking the source of the River Eden in 1664. Another pillar, at the river's mouth at Burgh Marsh on the Solway Firth, marks the death of Edward I in 1307 as he made camp with his army on his way to attack the Scots. Between the two, the Eden runs for 75 miles or so. Oozing through bleak boggy moorland from its source, it soon flows turbulently through the dramatic narrow ravine of Hellgill. Then its original southerly course switches abruptly and the river then flows northwards through Mallerstang, gushing through another gorge of eroded rocks near Kirkby Stephen. As the river reaches flatter land it slows and broadens, and flows peacefully past Appleby and a series of lovely villages with handsome red sandstone bridges. From Lazonby it assumes another character, with towering tree-topped bluffs and sandstone cliffs on either side. For a few miles the pace of the water quickens, the river flows restlessly over rapids until it reaches Wetheral where it slows once more. The Eden finally flows through Carlisle before meandering on a broad tidal course to the Solway Firth.

The Eden Valley itself is hard to define. Many consider it to be just the area around the River Eden in its central section, say from Brough to Wetheral. Others would argue it encompasses more. For the purposes of this book I have included Mallerstang and the Upper Eden Valley and, very roughly, the broader valley between the Lake District and the Pennines. I skipped Carlisle, but couldn't resist including the Eden as its waters finally mingle with the Border Esk in the great estuarial area of the Solway Firth. In truth I would be hard pressed to defend that expanse of wild flat tidal land as part of the Eden Valley.

Tourist literature understandably plays on the name Eden. 'Paradise' and 'idyll' are heavily overused words. Although it is an area blessed in many respects, people's lives are no doubt beset by similar problems as outside 'Eden'. Farmers battle with the weather and bureaucracy, villagers lack convenient services and people are faced with health and personal problems as anywhere else. Good it might be, but paradise it isn't!

Debates over the latest wind farms and supermarket developments tend to fill the front page of the local paper, the *Cumberland and Westmorland Herald*. People might grumble about how things are, but there is a general

LEFT The Scandal Beck rises on Wild Boar Fell and flows through the inviting valley of Smardale to join the Eden at Soulby. Smardale Gill is owned by the Cumbria Wildlife Trust and supports a wide range of plant, insect and river life. Apart from its wealth of natural history, the valley is rich in human history. There are the visible outlines of the round huts of Iron Age villages and cultivation terraces. Large oblong earth mounds, known as 'giants' graves', probably have a more mundane history. Other interesting remains are more recent. An impressive restored railway viaduct, which crosses high above the Scandal Beck, once carried trains on the now redundant north-east line from Teesside to Tebay. Nowadays it is the course of a favourite walk of mine. Starting from Smardale Hall on the track following the redundant line, the first point of interest is the railway viaduct carrying the Settle to Carlisle railway at the north end of the valley. The foundations of the spans go down 45 feet under ground in some instances – the engineers having mistakenly thought that they were building on secure bedrock, discovered it was actually red shale. The walk passes old railway cottages, quarries and lime kilns before crossing the old stone Smardale Bridge to the other side of the valley, returning to Smardale Hall over the fell.

LEFT Apple Day, held in October at the National Trust property of Acorn Bank is a lively occasion, with advice on growing apples, demonstrations of pruning, and plenty of apples to sample. In addition there are apple games, many stalls and entertainment by morris dancers.

OPPOSITE The Millenium Bridge at Stenkrith Park, Kirkby Stephen, is on the southern edge of the town alongside the narrow road bridge of Stonecroft on the minor road leading to Nateby. This attractive footbridge, designed in the Victorian style but actually made of galvanised steel, was opened in 2002 as part of the millennium celebrations. The breathtaking view over the ornate railings into the devilish chasm made by the River Eden below is not to be missed. This account by a travel writer was written in the early nineteenth century: *The water roars and gushes through the surrounding rocks and precipices with such violence, as almost to deafen the visitor. Three or four yards from the bridge is an immense abyss, where the waters 'incessantly roar', which goes by the name of Devil's Hole; the tradition of which is, that two lovers were swallowed up in this frightful gulf. The neighbouring peasants tell a tale of one Deville, a lover, who, through revenge, plunged his fair mistress into these waters.*

resistance to change. Not an awful lot actually does happen, and plenty of space in the paper is devoted to the doings of the WI, the local churches and cattle prices. The status quo rules, generally the boat is not rocked and it is no surprise that MPs from time immemorial have held huge Conservative majorities. Large country estates are still common and some, as a matter of regret, block public access to the River Eden, spoiling the ideal of a footpath following the river along its entire length. Notwithstanding, the area is well served by footpaths, many following age-old tracks and drove roads from village to village. Recently-created long-distance trails through the area include the Coast to Coast and Pennine Way.

Historically, artists and writers were drawn to the neighbouring Lake District. Wordsworth visited and wrote about the Eden Valley but his home, along with Ruskin, Coleridge and others was most definitely in the central Lakes. However, today the attractive landscape and quiet environment of the Eden Valley attracts artists, craftspeople and writers. It is significant that insufficient public money has ever been found to build a decent theatre or concert hall. Music and theatre happen as often as not in school or village halls. As with so much else, cultural activity exists on a scale that's small and personal.

Whichever way you look at it, the large village of Lazonby lies in the heart of the Eden Valley. It has an important auction mart where many thousands of sheep are sold in the autumn, a small craft shop making wooden toys and its own outdoor swimming pool. It also boasts a station on the Settle to Carlisle railway line and one of the most impressive sandstone bridges across the Eden. However, my usual reason for stopping at Lazonby is to shop at the large Co-op store that serves many surrounding smaller villages. A favourite game of mine is to spot how many people are wearing muddy wellies. I'm not talking about posh Hunter wellies, just common or garden muddy wellies. People lead lives that involve mucky clothes, and very mucky boots and wouldn't dream of changing them to go shopping. And the Co-op doesn't bat an eyelid. It sums up something I love about the Eden Valley – its lack of pretension. Unlike the Cotswolds, and dare I say it, the south generally, there are mercifully few, if any, shops dedicated to selling trivia, trowels with flowery handles, gardening aprons and the like.

Driving round the network of remote lanes between Lazonby and the Pennines I half expect to get stuck in traffic – but the traffic is likely to be a muck spreader or a Land Rover towing a trailer load of sheep on the way to market. The landscape of this deeply rural area is a living one, moulded by farming activity. Rolling fields bounded by red sandstone walls, with mixed crops and cattle are interspersed with small barns and woodlands. It is a richly varied and attractive landscape. While modern farming only employs small numbers of people (the public sector is the biggest employer) its significance in maintaining the traditional appearance of the Eden Valley is huge. To some extent the future prosperity of the area, in particular the tourist industry, is dependent on farming. Change that landscape and fewer tourists may visit –

but it's a delicate balance. Improving access and amenities, or creating specific tourist attractions might irreversibly damage the intrinsic appeal of this quiet and traditional pastoral landscape. A general preference for the small scale, a tendency to maintain traditions, to keep to the status quo might not be just the way things have tended to be in the Eden Valley but the way things should stay in the future. Being backward to go forward!

As I look back over the quarter of a century and more that I have lived with my distant view across the Eden Valley to Cross Fell, I reflect on what has happened in that passage of time. Aside from the two largest towns, Penrith and Carlisle, visible changes have been modest. Small scale, generally discreet housing developments have been built in many Eden Valley villages. A smattering of village schools and shops have closed. Sad to say, local delivery vans have often been displaced by Tesco vans. The main roads are far busier but many more cyclists enjoy the quiet back roads. Nunnery Walks, a great favourite of mine, was closed a few years back. On a positive note the Watermill at Little Salkeld and the Village Bakery at Melmerby thrive, as do an increasing number of organic producers for small food businesses. Earlier threats to close Acorn Bank Garden and the Settle to Carlisle Railway were lifted. On the personal front my two daughters grew up and left to study and then work in cities, symptomatic of this rural area. I miss them but I trust their northern roots will stay with them.

My work as a freelance photographer has grown way beyond anything I ever dreamt. The introduction of computers and the internet has been hugely important for me as must be the case for the many working from home in the Eden Valley, where broadband projects made a major impact. Above all, over nearly half a lifetime I have felt deeply rooted in an area that has also been a source of photographic inspiration.

BELOW **The limestone pavement of Great Asby is one of the best examples of its kind in Britain and is a National Nature Reserve. The wholesale removal of limestone pavement for use in garden rockeries has ruined these exceptional habitats in some surrounding areas, so protection is vital. The large blocks of stone are called clints and are riven with fissures called grikes. These damp and shaded deep clefts have a growing environment similar to that of a woodland floor and many unusual plants thrive in this upland habitat, including two scarce ferns; the rigid buckler fern and the limestone fern.**

The magical light of the Lake District may be somewhat lacking from the Eden Valley and its rolling curves are less easy to photograph than the Lake District valleys, nevertheless there are compensations. Great photographic subjects include the long line of the Pennine summits with their curiously pointed out-lying pikes, the valley of Mallerstang deeply enclosed within its spectacular edges and the ruined castles which remain as evidence of the area's violent earlier history. I have to admit it is also a relief not to be one of a horde of photographers as happens so easily in the Lakes! The Eden Valley remains overshadowed – in every way – by its hugely popular neighbour but I find its subtle appeal deeply rewarding.

RIGHT **Cattle herded along an ancient sunken lane leading towards Church Brough.**

BELOW **Although sheep are predominant, the Eden Valley is characterised by mixed agriculture. This patchwork of fields in rolling scenery with cows, sheep and crops interspersed with small woodlands, is typical of the rural scenery around Ainstable.**

ABOVE Brough, originally from the word 'fortification', is split by the A66 dual carriageway. All that most drivers will register as they speed past is the impressive ruin of Brough Castle. Market Brough lies on the other side, but the smaller settlement of Church Brough has both the castle and the large church. The church has a leper's squint, where those afflicted could take Mass without contaminating the rest of the congregation.

BELOW Pendragon Castle is strategically placed above the River Eden in Mallerstang. It was believed to have been founded by Uther Pendragon, the father of King Arthur. A gruesome legend tells of Uther being killed here along with a hundred of his men when the Saxon invaders poisoned the well. The earlier wooden structure was replaced in the mid-twelfth century by a stone building with one of the largest keeps in the north of England. This rebuilding was probably the work of the Norman knight Hugh de Morville. Legend has it that he left the castle after feeling spooked; an outline of Wild Boar Fell as seen from the castle window resembled an archbishop lain on his side complete with beard and a mitre. De Morville, who was complicit in the murder of St Thomas à Beckett, believed it was his ghost come back to haunt him. The castle has a chequered history of repeated attacks by Scottish raiders and subsequent restoration. Women twice restored it from ruin; the first was Lady Idonea de Veteripont in the fourteenth century, the second was in the seventeenth century, after yet another burning, when Lady Anne Clifford restored it to its full magnificence and also built the bridge over the Eden nearby. Thereafter the castle once again lay abandoned and in ruins.

spring

Spring can be a testing time in the far north of England. Warm days, heady with the promise of the new season and better weather, are replaced by wearying periods of grey skies and bitter winds when we wonder if spring will ever arrive. Then the clocks change and the season gradually becomes more established. The hedges quicken with the fresh green of new leaves and the snowy blossom of the blackthorn. Yellow celandines open their petals to the sunshine. Lacklustre grass in the fields slowly greens up and recovers from its late winter drabness while the persistent bleating of sheep calling their new lambs fill the air. The cuckoo's repetitive call and the welcome sight of the returning swallows and house martins swooping around their northern homes put the final seal on spring. Snow may yet fall on the high ground of the Pennines and indeed has been known to fall in the summer but on the valley floor winter has been finally banished.

RIGHT **Lambs and their mothers laze in the dappled sunshine, beneath spring apple blossom. Appropriately the photo was taken in Appleby, which means 'farmstead with an apple tree'.**

BELOW Near Crosby Ravensworth a bank of primroses heralds spring. Before long the ground will be flecked with white blossom drifting down from the canopy of hawthorn trees above.

ABOVE Green lanes, like this one leading towards Church Brough, are surely one of the most pleasant ways of exploring the Eden Valley. Colloquially these hedge-lined lanes are known as 'lonnings' (a northern word for lane) and would likely have been often used for herding cattle. They certainly still are today. The unfolding views of Brough Castle when walking along the lane are particularly good, with Stainmore offering a fine backdrop.

LEFT An early sight in spring are the curious flower spikes of butterbur along the damp sandy beaches bordering the River Eden. The leaves generally come after the flower and grow into huge umbrella shapes, the largest leaves of any British plant when fully grown. The name derives from their early use, to wrap butter.

The Ais Gill cascades down the limestone ravine of White Kirk on the lower slopes of Wild Boar Fell, before joining forces with Hell Gill Beck and flowing northwards through Mallerstang as the River Eden.

LEFT The Eden, called Hell Gill Beck at this point, is still very much newborn when it has its first grown up moment and runs through a dramatic ravine before plunging over this cliff at Hell Gill Force.

RIGHT The River Eden sweeps round a broad bend just before Wetheral. At this point the shelves of sandstone lying just underneath the shallow water are particularly evident and a succession of little red sandy beaches border the riverbank.

LEFT General wisdom has it that cowslips are becoming increasingly rare. However, around the Eden Valley, especially on the well drained limestone, they are still commonplace. Roadside verges in particular are transformed into natural spring gardens.

RIGHT Daffodils herald the end of winter beside the River Eden near Kirkoswald. This is the time of the year when grass often looks at its most drab, in contrast to the radiance of the yellow daffodils.

BELOW A wonderful display of snowdrops seen on a bank above a little oxbow in the splendidly named Crowdundle Beck, one of the Eden's many feeder streams that run down from the Pennine heights. The woodland is just behind Acorn Bank and red squirrels can often be seen here.

Morland Beck passes peacefully over a ford and under a wooden footbridge. A little further downstream it cascades over a waterfall overlooked by a café and then flows through the grounds of Morland Hall, where the interesting historic gardens are open to the public.

BELOW St Laurence's Church in Morland is particularly fine. The tower is believed to be Saxon and with its thick walls and tiny window slits would have been an ideal shelter during the turbulent times to come.

ABOVE I always thought it a bit unlikely, but this tower atop a steep little hill in Kirkoswald is actually the church tower. The main church, St Oswald's, nestles below and is built on the site of a spring that was worshipped in pre-Christian times. The spring still flows and a little flight of steps on the east side of the church leads down to a well. A small metal drinking cup, conveniently attached by a chain, can be let down into the well – the water drawn up tastes so good!

LEFT St Oswald's well.

ABOVE The woods along the River Eden at Wetheral,
owned by the National Trust, were badly affected by
Dutch elm disease. However the extra light benefited
the wild flowers. Campion, bluebells and wild garlic
grow in profusion on this particular bank.

OPPOSITE This ancient lane, hollowed out by centuries of
use, leads down to the River Eden near Kirkby Stephen
at Swingy Bridge.

LEFT Spring flowers blossom in the front gardens of the sandstone houses along Boroughgate in Appleby.

RIGHT Mayday in Melmerby and the villagers turn out on the village green to celebrate. The May Queen dances around the maypole while the Penrith Town Band marches past. Flocks of geese are used to graze the extensive green and their feathers were used in the village's pillow and mattress industry.

BOTTOM FAR RIGHT The Penrith Town Band.

BOTTOM RIGHT Dufton lies on the Pennine Way and is without doubt one of the most picturesque villages in the Eden Valley. Attractive red sandstone houses border the village green, which is split diagonally by a handsome avenue of lime trees. On this occasion, chicken racing, as well as an egg hunt on the green, was an Easter Sunday treat, drawing a small enthusiastic crowd. As far as I could see no bets were placed, which is perhaps just as well, as most chickens managed to escape the netted run and spent the rest of the afternoon being chased around the village green evading capture.

ABOVE These curious ridges on the further hillside, here side-lit by the sun, are evidence of early cultivation. Long strip terraces, known as lynchets, such as these near Great Musgrave, can be seen in various sites around the upper Eden Valley and are evidence that crops have been grown in this area from very early times.

ABOVE Ewes and their lambs approached me, hoping that my camera bag contained something interesting. Sadly I had to disappoint them! The little lane in the background leads to the pretty hamlet of Greenwell near Castle Carrock in the far north of the Eden Valley.

The views from Mallerstang Edge are spectacular. The evocative moorland calls of curlews and lapwings fill the air in this lonely spot. Looking south the view is into Yorkshire, where the limestone peaks of Whernside and Ingleborough can be seen on the horizon. The views to the north-west are across the Eden Valley to the Pennine chain. However, one step too close to the rim would mean a fearsome drop over the sheer cliffs into the valley below.

OPPOSITE **Wild Boar Fell in Mallerstang** is a real geological hotchpotch. This limestone pavement lies half way up the slopes. The mountain's base is sandstone and shale, but it is capped with millstone grit forming the dramatic escarpment of the Nab, part of the summit ridge of Wild Boar Fell that can be seen in the photo.

ABOVE **Early risers from congregations of the Churches of Appleby and Orton** gather at dawn on Easter Sunday for a 'sonrise' service to celebrate Easter Sunday. Interestingly, the location is on Raise Howe, an ancient tumulus that might well have seen pre-Christian ceremonies.

gardens

The fertility of the Eden Valley soil lends itself naturally to gardening, and it is hard to resist invoking the words 'the gardens of Eden'. The area has an abundance of beautiful traditional English gardens, largely (and thankfully!) untroubled by the vagaries of current garden fashions. The climate is quite a bit drier than the Lake District, though the fellside villages along the foot of the Pennines have to contend with occasional blasts from the vicious Helm Wind. In summer, several villages have a 'garden trail' weekend, which is a great chance to be nosy.

RIGHT **Corby Castle, a Grade I listed thirteenth-century building with seventeenth and eighteenth-century additions, overlooks the River Eden. It is not open to the public, but one of the most spectacular parts of the garden can be seen across the River Eden at Wetheral. This impressive cascade flows from a temple, through the gaping jaws of mythical beasts. A statue of Nelson stands by the pool at the base.**

LEFT The gardens of Morland Hall, with their strong Victorian atmosphere, are open to visitors to the shop and the lovely café. Little bridges criss-cross the river and there is a small grotto by the waterfall. A former limestone quarry is interestingly planted.

BELOW LEFT The lovely garden at Greencroft House in Great Strickland opens for private visits. The garden is divided into a number of strikingly different 'rooms'. The owner, an artist, is particularly adept at creating a gorgeous palette of colours.

ABOVE **Hazel Cottage**, just outside Armathwaite, extends to just over 5 acres and includes an interesting area of planting along an old railway line, with garden pools and bridges, and great banks of candelabra primulas in the spring. It opens under the National Garden Scheme.

RIGHT **Nunwick Hall**, close to Great Salkeld, opens on occasions for charity and private groups. It has a highly productive and attractive walled kitchen garden as well as a large Victorian grotto.

LEFT **Winderwath**, near Temple Sowerby, opens regularly and any lover of plant 'specials' would particularly enjoy this garden. Plants include trilliums, unusual arisaemas, and an extensive range of uncommon alpines.

summer

The gentle pace of life in the Eden Valley slips into a slightly higher gear in the summer. Unlike the Lake District, which will have been teeming with visitors since Easter (not to mention teeming with rain!), the largely uncommercial villages and market towns of the Eden Valley comfortably accommodate a smattering of discerning tourists. It is a relaxed area for 'saints and sinners' – the rewarding combination of visiting one of the atmospheric country churches followed by a lazy lunch outside a nearby pub. Those with an alternative bent can join the midsummer day dawn gathering at the Bronze Age stone circle, Long Meg and her Daughters. Weekly steam trains run along the Carlisle to Settle line passing through some of the best valley scenery, and the leisurely village festivals, garden openings and local shows fill the dog days of summer. An exception is the annual Appleby Horse Fair in early June, when many thousands of visitors flood to the little town. Tranquillity soon returns.

RIGHT **Swathes of pink thrift bloom in May on the salt marshes bordering the Solway, where the tidal estuaries of the Border Esk and Eden converge in a vast unspoilt seascape. Winding drainage creeks cut through the 'merse', filling to the brim and often overflowing at high tide, while at low tide the slicks of their oozing muddy sides gleam in the light.**

Most traditional herb meadows have been converted into productive grassland but Mallerstang and the upper Eden Valley are blessed in still having a good number of traditionally managed hay meadows with their wonderful displays of wild flowers in summer. Yellow rattle, pignut, wood cranesbill, lady's mantle and buttercup grow in colourful profusion. The meadows are not cut until July or August and then grazed by cattle in the autumn and spring.

PREVIOUS PAGE **Clouds of golden pollen rose from the heather as I pushed past it on this August day. The view across the heather moorland above Crosby Ravensworth is to Cross Fell and the Pennines in the far distance. This very remote stone monument is called Black Dub and the inscription reads;**
Here at Black Dub
The Source of the Livennet
King Charles the II
Regaled his army
And drank of the water
On his march from Scotland
August 8 1651
Would there have been heather then, I wonder? If so, it would have been blooming on that date.

ABOVE **Herons on the Solway shoreline hoping for an evening catch. The mountain of Criffel, on the Scottish coast on the far side of the Solway, rises in the distance.**

BELOW Haaf netting on the Solway is an age-old fishing method used to catch salmon as they make their way to and from the river of their birth. Haaf means 'sea net', and probably derives from Norse as this fishing practice came across with the Vikings. Today the fishermen of the Solway jealously guard their right to fish with the nets, despite some doubts from the Environment Agency which regulates the licences. The incoming Solway tide advances at an alarming speed and the fishermen with their line of nets need to keep moving inshore or else get out of their depth. With the soft sands of the estuary, I wouldn't like to be the one on the far end of the line!

Well Tree Cottage is in an idyllic spot on the River Lyvennet, just below King's Meaburn. Lyvennet means 'the smooth sliding or slippery one'. The footbridge next to this cottage fortunately avoids any need to walk cross the adjacent ford, that I know from experience can itself be treacherously slippery.

ABOVE Mist floats above every dip and hollow on this midsummer dawn morning. The view is across the expanse of the Eden Valley to Cross Fell and the line of the Pennines beyond.

ABOVE **The gently undulating Eden Valley landscape
to the west of Church Brough, lit by evening sun.**

LEFT The churchyard of St Mary's, the little church in Mallerstang, is knee deep in frothy pignut in late May. According to the inscribed stone above the porch, this church was yet another restoration by the indefatigable Lady Anne Clifford, in 1663, at a cost of £46 15s. In addition, she bought land to provide an income for a teacher. One sad memorial in the churchyard is to the twenty-five workmen (and some of their families) who died in the bleak living and working conditions while the Mallerstang section of the Settle to Carlisle railway was being built.

BELOW LEFT Outhgill in Mallerstang is a hamlet with only a dozen or so houses. One of these was once the home of the father of Michael Faraday. His son subsequently rose to eminence as a scientist, in particular as the inventor of the dynamo. His father, the local blacksmith, moved to London in the year of Michael's birth, but relatives remained in Kirkby Stephen, which now has a Faraday Street.

LEFT Crosby Garrett is in limestone country and the light grey stone buildings of the west of the Eden Valley contrast with the red sandstone further east. The fell beyond was populated in prehistoric times and there is evidence in abundance of Bronze Age cairns and stone circles and very early hut dwellings. The small village church crowns an extremely steep artificial mound – from which this photo was taken. Historically this mound served a defensive purpose. The sight of beacons lit to the north warned the women and children of the village to take refuge in the church, against another attack from border raiders. The church's interior is impressive, with Norman arches and pillars. The viaduct at the back of the village carries the Settle to Carlisle railway line.

RIGHT **Little Salkeld is** best known for its working watermill, restored in 1975, and now one of the few country corn mills using water power to grind flour. A variety of different flours are produced using traditional French burr millstones and organic British wheat. Visitors to the watermill can watch the two overshot waterwheels in action and tours inside the mill are available. But perhaps the very best bit is saved until last, going to the tearoom to enjoy the tasty baked goods made with the flour milled next door.

BELOW RIGHT **Maulds** Meaburn is one of those pretty, unspoilt villages that so characterise the Eden Valley. Meaburn, which means 'stream through the meadows', could justly have had the appendage 'surrounded by attractive cottages with a lovely arched stone bridge and wooden footbridge'. 'Mauld' comes from Maud de Morville who, with her brother, owned the medieval manor which included Maulds (Maud's) Meaburn and what is now King's Meaburn. Her brother, Hugh de Morville, lived at Pendragon Castle and was one of the knights involved in the killing of Thomas à Becket. For this he forfeited his share of the estate to the Crown. Maud retained her share, but the northern part took the name of King's Meaburn.

RIGHT The iron footbridge that adjoins the Carlisle to Newcastle railway as it crosses high above the River Eden at Wetheral on the very lofty viaduct should be strictly avoided by anyone prone to vertigo. However it affords this wonderful view north, encompassing the pastoral scenery around Warwick Bridge and beyond, towards the Bewcastle Fells in the far north of Cumbria. The footpath also links Wetheral to Great Corby, on the east side of the Eden, avoiding what would otherwise be a tedious detour on roads via Warwick Bridge. A set of ninety-one steps leading steeply down to the river on the Wetheral side is constructed from the solid stone sleepers from the old railway line, which were replaced with wooden sleepers.

BOTTOM **Rutter Mill was once a working watermill.** In its working life it had various uses, from a bobbin mill, a corn mill and then a timber mill. The Great Asby Electric Light and Water Company installed a turbine in 1928 but it was never a reliable source of electricity. Rutter Force is impressive after heavy rain and may then justify its name, which probably comes from the old English word *hrutere*, meaning 'to roar'. Ducks are often busy dabbling away in the water under the footbridge or on the ford, adding to the charm of this pretty corner of the Eden Valley.

BELOW Appleby Horse Fair takes place at the beginning of June. 'Fair Hill', on the edge of the town, becomes home for a week for the many travellers who come from across northern England. Showy modern motor-drawn caravans far outnumber the decorative traditional Romany caravans, or vardos. The fair doesn't meet with universal approval, bringing with it a share of drunken brawls and vast quantities of litter, rather detracting from the romantic notion of a gypsy fair. However, the primary purpose of horse trading goes on apace. Here, the washing of horses in the River Eden is a preliminary to galloping them up and down a lane, to display them at their best, hoping to attract the attention of potential buyers.

A group of three Romany caravans make their way along the
quiet road through Mallerstang to the Appleby Horse Fair.

FAR LEFT St Stephen's Church overlooks Kirkby Stephen's market square. The main entrance is through the cloisters which originally housed a butter market. The pediment and bellcote add to their character. Between the market square and the River Eden are several narrow winding passageways, and one of these, Stoneshot, has a network of tunnels built beneath. There are many theories as to their purpose, but it seems likely that they were either used for shelter during the Scottish border raids or for the moving of beer barrels.

LEFT The High Cross Pillar marks the top of Boroughgate, Appleby's lovely tree-lined sloping main street that leads downhill from the castle gates. The Low Cross, shown above, which is similar, is in the market place by the cloisters of St Lawrence's Church. The High Cross has the inscription *Retain your loyalty, Preserve your rights*, thought to celebrate the restoration of Charles II.

OPPOSITE Appleby, or Appleby-in-Westmorland as it is more precisely known, was the ancient county town of Westmorland. Although local government reorganisation merged Cumberland and Westmorland into Cumbria, Appleby's determination not to let the name Westmorland be eradicated can only be applauded. It has its own town council, with four aldermen and mayor. The wonderfully characterful council chamber, hung with portraits of former mayors, is a model of civic pride. One former alderman was Jack Robinson, who rose from humble beginnings to considerable eminence and became an MP. In 1763 he built the White House, which has lovely ogee windows, and is more divertingly referred to as 'the house that Jack built'. William Pitt was another MP, put forward for the seat of Appleby in 1781 by Sir James Lowther, and so began his life in Parliament.

BELOW LEFT Stainton Show is held in the grounds of Hutton-in-the-Forest, a stately home a few miles north of Penrith, in August. Here a judge is about to check the teeth on this blue-faced Leicester ram. This breed was developed in Cumbria and Northumberland and the sheep are very distinctive with their long Roman noses. I've always enjoyed the way the expression on the judge's face mirrors that of the sheep.

BELOW RIGHT Today's shepherds are likely to use aluminium crooks, but these beautiful handmade traditional sticks are displayed at the summer agricultural shows. The crook shape enabled shepherds to catch their sheep around the neck.

The tradition of rushbearing is still observed in Great Musgrave and Warcop. The ceremony originated when churches had earth floors, and sweet smelling new rushes were cut and laid each summer. Nowadays it is a simple village flower festival, with decorated crowns being worn by the girls, and rush crosses carried by the boys. A church service is followed by tea in the village hall and rounded off by sports. I like this photo, below, where the team leader appears to be meeting some resistance!

The warm sandstone of the lovely and ancient church at Edenhall is lit by summer evening sunshine. The dedication to St Cuthbert is one of several in Cumbria. The saint preached in Cumbria in the seventh century and became the Bishop of Lindisfarne in nearby Northumberland. It is possible that the church was built on a resting spot for the saint's remains when they were taken to Lindisfarne for burial. The battlemented little tower would no doubt have served a defensive role.

LEFT The late glow of evening midsummer sun casts across this tarn with its splendid backdrop of Wild Boar Fell.

BELOW LEFT A beautiful early autumn evening looking across from the countryside around Ainstable to the distant fells of the Lake District, with the unmistakable outline of Blencathra.

LEFT **A warm evening in midsummer when the sun sets towards the north over the Solway Firth. The last of the sun casts a rich glow, slanting sideways across the gently undulating scenery of the Eden Valley.**

LEFT The peaty waters of the Croglin Beck surge dramatically down a narrow gorge on the final leg of its short journey before it runs into the River Eden. Spectacular waterfalls abound and the noise of the crashing water is amplified by the surrounding sandstone cliffs. This final turbulent course of the stream was laid out in the mid-eighteenth century as a picturesque landscape, known as Nunnery Walks. Steps, viewing platforms and a summerhouse remain in place. A circular path, once open to the public, led excitingly along an edge eroded into low cliffs along the River Eden. Like many other people, this was our top spot for a family outing in the Eden Valley. Lamentably the property has recently been closed to the public.

TOP RIGHT Fly-fishing a team of wet flies in the tail of one of the long pools near Armathwaite. The River Eden has yielded some of the largest salmon ever caught in England, and 15–20 lb salmon start their run in August, the main run being in the autumn. On their return upriver they don't feed, relying on their fat stocks from their North Atlantic feeding grounds. However, they are still ready to jump at an angler's lure on their home run. No one knows why.

BOTTOM RIGHT The River Eden weaves its way through every channel in the beautifully eroded brockram bedrock of Stenkrith Park in Kirkby Stephen. Brockram is curious; it consists of limestone fragments within sandstone. The birdlife is rich here and dippers fly at top speed low along the water or zip endlessly from rock to rock, settling just long enough to bob up and down a time or two, before they're off again skimming along the river on their perpetual pursuit of insects.

henges and circles

BELOW It always struck me as odd that a road, albeit a very quiet farm lane, should run through Long Meg and her Daughters, one of the finest stone circles in the country. Wordsworth described the henge as being second only to Stone Henge, and certainly it is one of the largest stone circles in Britain. Long Meg, an outlier, is the tallest of the stones and made of sandstone, whereas the sixty-five or so 'daughters' are granite. Stone axes crafted in Langdale would likely have been used in the construction. The height and position of the 'mother' stone of Long Meg might just have been placed to help travellers locate the circle. However, it was probably deliberately aligned with the midwinter sunset as seen from the centre of the circle. Little ritualistic tokens, left by today's solstice worshippers, hang from the trees along the lane.

BOTTOM The number of henges in relatively close proximity is an indication of the size of the Neolithic population of the area. The stucture of Mayburgh Henge at Eamont Bridge is unusual; its single circular bank is made from pebbles from the River Eamont, rather than the spoil from a surrounding ditch. This single stone is probably part of a stone circle, or even two, existing within the henge.

lady anne clifford

Lady Anne Clifford was a brilliant Eden Valley benefactress. Born in 1590, she was for much of her upbringing at the court of Elizabeth I. The only surviving child of her father, George Clifford, 3rd Earl of Cumberland, she was deprived of her inheritance when on his death his titles and estates went instead to his brother. She battled for many years for her inheritance but only succeeded when her uncle died without heirs and she finally inherited the 90,000 acres of the Clifford Estates. Six years later, following the end of the English Civil War, and at the age of sixty, she moved north to spend her remaining twenty-seven years restoring the estates, which had suffered from centuries of border raids and the civil war. Lady Anne would travel between her castles – Skipton and Barden Tower in Yorkshire, Brougham, Appleby, Brough and Pendragon in the Eden Valley – with a huge procession of forty or more carts. They transported all manner of things for her needs, including her bed and a pane of glass for her bedroom window. Lady Anne herself was carried in a litter. The entourage must have made an odd site, coming over the rough moorland route from Yorkshire, on a track that is known as Lady Anne's Way. It is hard to travel far in the Eden Valley from Penrith southwards without coming across an example of her philanthropy, and we have much to thank her for, particularly in her restoration of so many of the lovely churches in the area. In addition she set a great example; indomitable, independent, highly cultured and intelligent – and she loved the north!

TOP RIGHT **The tiny, remote Church of Ninekirks, or St Ninians, is rarely used, and is cared for by the Churches Conservation Trust. It is still consecrated, and was decorated on this occasion for a summer wedding when the guests arrived through the surrounding fields on foot. Fittingly, the church has a romantic location, in a corn field bounded by a curve in the River Eamont. Built on the site of an ancient cell occupied by the early missionary St Ninian, Ninekirks was later one of Lady Anne Clifford's restorations and was typical of the unshowy style she favoured. Her restoration work is recorded in the plasterwork above the altar, in a wreath with her initials A P (Anne Pembroke, the Earl of Pembroke being her second husband). The church remains almost unaltered since then.**

CENTRE RIGHT **Lady Anne's Pillar lies on the border of Yorkshire and Cumbria and on the watershed of Britain, a true divide between east and west. Nearby is the source of the Ure, flowing east, and the Eden, flowing west. The Pillar, erected by Lady Anne, unlike the many other cairns on the surrounding fells, is built of squared off stones. Once ruinous, it was restored in 1953. The views in nearly every direction are outstanding. The source of the Eden itself lacks romance. Water oozes from one pool to another and in the soggy morass it is not easy to identify the very first gurgle. However, the exhilaration of being in such remote country, with only the company of a golden plover flitting just ahead from one marshy bank to another, is a reward for the long climb.**

BOTTOM RIGHT **Brougham Castle, on the site of a key Roman fort by the River Eamont, was built in the late thirteenth century and later strengthened with a double gatehouse to withstand the border raids. It was damaged in the English Civil War and then restored by Lady Anne.**

autumn

This is the time for the major sheep gatherings from the high slopes of the Pennines and the big autumn sheep sales provide a chance for farmers to get together and chew the fat on sheep prices and the ups and downs of that farming year. Salmon fishing on the Eden reaches its peak as the main run of fish return to their birthplaces. Hedgerows provide rich pickings of blackberries, sloes and elderberries, and red squirrels make short work of burying hazelnuts. Harvest festivals are celebrated in churches, and villagers gather in halls for harvest suppers, significant traditional events in this agricultural area.

RIGHT **A pair of swans glide silently across a tarn on Brackenber Moor, near Appleby. The last of the late autumn evening sun lights up the reedy shore and Hilton Pike. Elsewhere on Brackenber Moor the turf is manicured – it is the site of one of the most scenic golf courses in Cumbria.**

At the end of autumn the group of farmers who have grazing rights around High Cup Nick spend a day gathering in all of their sheep for over-wintering in the valley. Once the sheep have been herded from the higher ground, they are penned lower down. Then the laborious process of sorting them out into their respective flocks begins. The fell resounds with the raucous din of the shouts of the farmers to their dogs and the agitated bleating of the great mass of sheep. It looks like sheer pandemonium but the sheep eventually get sorted into their respective flocks before being herded off homewards.

BELOW The first snows of winter in early November dust the top of High Cup Nick, the dramatic glacial valley, carved out of ancient ice into a perfect U-shape, rimmed with a stratum of exposed volcanic whinstone. The 'Nick' at the far end is actually Nichol's Chair, a pillar of rock rather than a nick in the rock wall. The story goes that Nichol was a local cobbler who, for reasons best known to himself, chose to climb the pinnacle and repair a pair of boots on the summit.

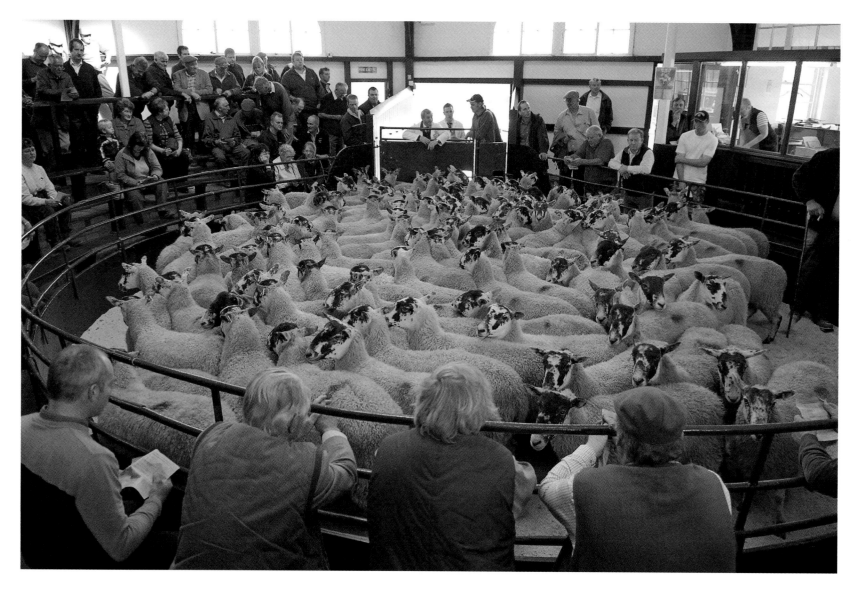

Lazonby Auction Mart attracts buyers from around the
country to its autumn sheep sales. This, the largest of
the autumn sales, is called the Harvest of the Fells and
is held in early October. During the course of the day,
up to 18,000 sheep change hands, most of them leaving
Cumbria to over-winter in the more lush pastures of
southern Britain. Visiting the upstairs café is, for me, like
entering another world, where the farming fraternity sit at
long tables discussing sheep prices and unceremoniously
wolf down huge fry ups and great slabs of cake. No one
bothers about mucky boots and overalls. It's great!

An early autumn morning by the River Eden near Lazonby
Bridge. Cows, taking their time, meander along the riverbank.

ABOVE The weir on the River Eden in Appleby provided
water for the millrace of Bongate Mill. Now a private
home, it was originally a corn mill with three waterwheels.
The adjacent lane, now deeply hollowed by erosion from
centuries of use, led to an important ford. The modern
Jubilee footbridge carries walkers across.

LEFT AND ABOVE The roaring waters of the weir at Armathwaite can be an awe-inspiring sight when the Eden is in spate following days of rain. When the flood waters start to recede and clear a little, the salmon choose their moment to make their autumn run up the river. There is a good chance of spotting them as they try to leap the tumbling waters of the weir on their return to their birth place.

ABOVE The impressive Norman keep of Caesar's Tower, rising above autumnal trees in the grounds of Appleby Castle. The site was well chosen, the keep occupying an excellent defensive position on high ground above a loop in the River Eden. Today, a flock of white doves wing their way back to the turrets, from where, no doubt, they will be keeping a defensive eye open for any predatory sparrowhawks. High Cup Nick looms in the far distance. Appleby Castle is the only Eden Valley castle restored by Lady Anne Clifford that didn't subsequently become ruinous. Sadly it is not open to the public.

ABOVE **An evening view in late October looking south along the River Eden from Armathwaite's handsome bridge. Armathwaite Castle, based on a four-storey pele tower, is on the right and now divided into flats. A lovely footpath, which starts by tucking underneath the bridge, leads upstream along the east bank to a weir.**

RIGHT We are very fortunate in the Eden Valley to be one of the very few places left in England where our native red squirrels still survive. Two organisations, Red Alert and the Penrith and District Red Squirrel Group, work to cull grey squirrels and improve the survival chances for the reds. Conservation areas have been designated, where the habitats particularly favour reds. Squirrel pox, carried by the greys but not lethal to them, sadly infects the reds, who can't survive it.

BELOW Seen against the shimmering backdrop of the River Eden in autumn, these beech trees blaze with colour while their dry leaves rustle in the wind. They border the broad riverside path at Armathwaite and are equally lovely in spring, with their fresh green leaves trembling in the breeze.

ABOVE **A group of horses led down to the River Eden at Appleby to be washed. Bongate Mill, clad in flame coloured creeper, was once a working corn mill. The raised water, held back by the weir, fed the millrace, which in turn drove the three identical waterwheels. The lane alongside once led to a ford, but a modern footbridge, built for the Jubilee, now serves walkers.**

Bonfire night on the broad village green of Milburn, one of the fellside villages tucked below the Pennines. The proceeds from the sale of warming soup, baked potatoes and sticky gingerbread – all welcome on a November night! – go towards the cost of the fireworks. Milburn is lucky as it still has a village school and the noise of children playing outside in their breaks brings animation to this normally quiet fellside village.

The sandstone houses make an almost perfect enclosure around the large village green, which is complete with a maypole. However, in a typical medieval plan, the four corners of the green were deliberately left open for the herding of sheep. The corners could be easily closed off to pen the sheep, or, if necessary to defend the village against marauders. Villagers still have grazing rights, and it is quite usual to see a tethered horse grazing the green.

sandstone

BELOW **Water flows smoothly over the eroded sandstone of the River Gelt, a northern tributary of the Eden. Gelt derives from 'mad' or 'wild' and, as it gushes through the Gelt Woods near Brampton, it truly lives up to its name.**

BOTTOM **These wonderful dogtooth or zig-zag carvings above the entrance to the church at Great Salkeld are Norman or earlier. Fortunately they are protected from the elements by a porch, leaving the soft sandstone little eroded. 'New red' Penrith sandstone is particularly warm.**

BELOW **This old quarry on the banks of the River Gelt was first mined by the Romans. Known as the Brampton Freestone Quarry, in more recent times it was worked by local people with commoner's rights.**

caves and carvings

The soft sandstone of the cliffs along the course of the River Eden has proved to be an invitation to carve curiosities. The ancient St Constantine's Cells, carved into the cliffs above the river at Wetheral, probably pre-date the Romans, but were later used by the nearby priory for hiding supplies away from the raiding Scots. Originally the only access was by a removable ladder and the entrance was well concealed. Steep stone steps leading to the caves are carved from a sandstone cliff wall, where a wealth of graffiti includes some by William Henry Mounsey, a wealthy Victorian romantic, who delighted in carving mysterious inscriptions using bardic script, Latin and a variety of symbols. His boldest creation, an inscription and strange moon faces, can be found on sandstone cliffs a little south of Armathwaite, only accessible when the River Eden is low.

BELOW **Lacy's Caves, set on a little bluff above the Eden, can be reached by walking a mile or so downstream from Little Salkeld. Lt. Col. Samuel Lacy of the Salkeld Hall Estate had them carved out of the sandstone in the eighteenth century, probably inspired by the fashion for romantic landscapes. He employed a hermit to add to the effect. The arched entrances lead to a surprisingly large and complex interior, with five interlinked chambers, and seats fashioned out of the rock.**

winter

I am not, I have to confess, a lover of winter, although plenty claim to be. However, walks on cold sunny days, when the chill nips the cheeks, temporarily persuade me otherwise. On very cold nights freezing fog rising above the River Eden creates hoar frosts, which by morning have transformed the trees and grasses along the riverbank, with a thick coating of white crystals. Snowfalls block the narrow lanes to the fellside villages, the drifting snow piling high against the stone walls. The savage Helm Wind howls its tormented course down the slopes of Cross Fell, blasting through the fellside villages and causing misery for days on end.

RIGHT **The clouds have been gradually lifting, but the summit of Cross Fell is not yet quite clear.**

BELOW The Lakeland Fells, dramatically silhouetted against the evening light seen from the top of the Hartside Pass. Blencathra, on the left, has the popular name of Saddleback, that distinctive shallow-cupped summit being easily identifiable when seen from the east.

LEFT **Surely one of the most dramatic moments on the Pennine Way is at High Cup Nick, overlooking the Eden Valley. Here a solitary walker, standing on a knife-edge, looks across the plunging valley.**

BELOW On this bitingly cold, stormy afternoon, rapidly moving shafts of sunlight flicker across the Eden Valley, with the Lakeland Fells as a backdrop. Rays of sunlight illuminate Knock and Dufton Pikes while passing snow showers temporarily obscure the view.

ABOVE **The view across the broad sweep of the Eden Valley, backed by the northern Lakeland Fells, as seen from the slopes of Cross Fell.**

PREVIOUS PAGE **The broad sweep of Cross Fell soars above the morning mist. The stubble remaining from last year's harvested crop will soon be ploughed in and the seeds sown for next summer's planting.**

ABOVE **I watched these starlings near Temple Sowerby one late afternoon in winter, congregating and making their wonderful swirling cloud formations, as they prepared to settle at their roosting site.**

LEFT Winter on the Solway, despite its savage and merciless winds, is the best season to visit and witness the great spectacle of over-wintering birds. Huge numbers of birds, such as these knots, assemble in late autumn and can be seen wheeling in tight flocks, making wonderful, twisting formations. The waders arrive early and feed on the mud and sand flats exposed by the vast tides. They are best seen on an incoming tide, where they progressively feed closer and closer to the shoreline, until the highest tide may drive them to an inland roost.

BELOW The winter evening view along the River Eamont, close to Watersmeet where it flows in to the River Eden. Gulls and lapwings are flying to their evening roost.

The cairns of Nine Standards Rigg on Hartley Fell above Kirkby Stephen. The story goes that they were built to fool attackers, as they resemble an advancing army. However it is more likely that they are boundary markers between Westmorland and Yorkshire.

BELOW The view from Hartside across the snow covered patchwork of fields and gentle undulations of the Eden Valley. The layer of snow accentuates the contours of the northern Lakeland Fells in the far distance. Blencathra, towards the left, is flanked on the right by the lesser known peaks of Bowscale, Carrock Fell and High Pike.

ABOVE **Wild Boar Fell**, with its millstone grit cap and steep escarpments rises above Mallerstang and looks particularly spectacular when snow covered. The double walls cutting across the lower slopes mark the track of the Settle to Carlisle railway, and the course of the infant River Eden can be made out as it threads its way between trees in the valley.

BELOW **A blizzard**, followed by a bit of snowmelt, has resulted in crazy contortions on this stone wall. The shadowed gulleys on Mallerstang Edge, on the right, show up especially well in the white snow.

ABOVE A gorgeous winter morning when white hoar frost crystals rimed every surface. The River Eamont, near Culgaith, flows into the Eden at this point, Watersmeet, after its short journey from Ullswater.

LEFT Fell ponies, well protected on this bitter evening by their thick winter coats, graze on the rough common behind Blencarn. Cross Fell rises in the distance.

BELOW A crisp winter morning looking across the
sandstone bridge crossing the Eden at Lazonby. The
unusual bell tower of St Oswald's Church at Kirkoswald is
perched on the hilltop, the church itself being out of view.
Haresceugh Fell rises in the distance.

ABOVE **This sandstone bridge across the river at Lazonby has to be my favourite Eden bridge. The previous night had seen dense freezing fog hanging over the river and had left every branch, twig, and stem of grass thickly rimed with sparkling hoar frost.**

BELOW These Swaledale sheep were on Hartside, watching for the daily arrival of the farmer with winter fodder. Ewes left on high ground will have gone to the 'tup' (ram) later in the autumn than those taken to the valley fields, so that the lambs are born on the fell when the main rigours of winter are past.

RIGHT Sheep pause their endless chewing of their winter feed of turnips for just a few seconds to give me the once over. Soon enough its noses to the ground again. Haze, backlit against the setting sun, produces a magical effect, complemented by the glinting River Eden.

eden benchmarchs and poetry path

'Eden Benchmarks' was created as a millennium project by the East Cumbria Countryside Project, who commissioned ten sculptors to each create a stone carving along the course of the River Eden. The sculptors were encouraged to be as creatively free as possible and the resulting benches are remarkably diverse.

By contrast, the twelve stones of the 'Poetry Path' are placed at intervals along a 2-mile circular walk by the River Eden at Kirkby Stephen. A series of short poems by Meg Peacocke celebrate each month of the hill farmer's year. The stones are beautifully carved with the poems and accompanying decorative motifs by Pip Hall.

TOP RIGHT **The May stone, on the subject of gathering and marking sheep:**
Penned in a huddle, the great tups
are clints of panting stone. The shepherd lifts
a sideways glance from the labour
of dagging tails. His hands are seamed with muck
and the sweat runs into his eyes.
Above us, a silent plane has needled
the clear blue. Paling behind it
a crimped double strand of wool unravels.

BOTTOM RIGHT **The January stone, on the subject of hedge laying:**
The sky's harsh crystal,
wind a blade, trees stripped,
grass dull with cold. Life
is a kernel hidden
in the stone of winter.

ABOVE *Red River* by Victoria Brailsford, at Temple Sowerby.

LEFT Mary Bourne's sculpture, *Water Cut*, is placed on a dramatic site, on the route of Lady Anne's Highway in Mallerstang. The River Eden rises nearby and the waving line created between the two stones represents the onwards course of the river, which can be seen winding on its northwards course in the valley below.

index